Is Anybody Listening?

Opal Belieu

NEWMAN SPRINGS PUBLISHING
320 Broad Street
Red Bank, NJ 07701

First originally published by Newman Springs Publishing 2020

ISBN 978-1-63692-200-3 (Paperback)
ISBN 978-1-63881-160-2 (Hardcover)
ISBN 978-1-63692-201-0 (Digital)

Printed in the United States of America

To my darling Mr. B, who really and truly is the other half of me; and to my sister, Doodlebug, to whom I know I can tell anything; and to my BFF Tonya, who I know has my back come what may.

Contents

The Rewards

To show love and to give love is the greatest gift that we can share; I know we all can do this, because that is why God put us all here.

We are here on this Earth to learn lessons and in turn create kindness and love; it is a gift that came so long ago from our Savior up above.

Although Jesus showed us some of his gifts as he traveled throughout the lands, he spoke of his Father's undying and never-ending love, if we would just hold on to his hand.

I choose to follow Jesus and give all that is asked of me, because my rewards are in heaven and someday they might be visible to me.

I know that I'm not good enough yet there for I have a long way to go; I just hope you follow a good path for your life, and this is something that I felt you should know.

(September 10, 2011)

Angel

There's an angel on my shoulder and it is watching over me; I can't really see or hear him for he is as quiet as can be.

I know I was meant for heaven because I've already been through hell.

I don't know if my angel is a female or a male, but I know he comes from heaven beyond the wispy veil.

Sometimes when I falter and path grows too wide, I call upon my angel because in God's love we do abide.

For I am in his and his love is in me, because God's Love is always where I want to be.

I know my angel will guide me under God's most precious wings for he speaks to me of Love and many other special things.

So, my friends, if you need an angel to guide you in truth and love, just look to the sky for your angel is above!

(September 24, 2011)

My Father Who Loves Me

Father God, please take away the spooky things that scare me in the night and cradle me in your loving arms until dawn's early light.

Father, please take away the fears that plague me each and every day; show me how to love you, Father, and teach me how to pray.

Show me how to love you, Father, and give to you as much as I can give then, now, and forever I may live. My love for you is never-ending and always will be for as long as I live.

Let me honor thy father and thy mother so that my days may be long in the land for I feel the second coming may be close at hand.

But to you let me always honor and glorify your name; if it pleases my Lord and you love me as I do you then please take away my shame.

I love you, Father, from your earthly daughter, who wrote this to bring you joy and laughter.

(February 6, 2012)

Just a Little Ditty

Lord, when the world I live in seems ominous and the sky above turns to gray, I only have to open my eyes to see the beauty that you've made.

And just like when the seasons all change and it seems like your love for me is out of range, I just have to look up to the sky and know you have a plan for me, even if I know not where, when, or why.

But every day I see your love abounding in the smallest of things and that keeps me astounded.

Never doubt my faith in you, though sometimes my religion may be tested, for it is in you that I give everything to, and that is when I feel totally rested.

I hope I don't pray too much, because I come to you with every small problem, especially when I myself cannot find an answer, but you always guide me on the right path, and you make me feel like dancer.

I know that you are right here.

So when my life gets too much for me to bear, whether it be good things or bad things, Father, I know that you are always right here.

Not only do you hold my hand but you lift my spirits high; that is why I adore you so much because you are my pie in the sky.

Not only are you the Alpha and Omega, the beginning and the end, I know I can trust in you and within everything because you are also my best friend.

(January 8, 2012)

Admiration

When the world outside is so harsh and all the world seems so lost and frustrated, Christians around the earth get up and sing praises and show God how much he is appreciated.

People, gather up your crosses and all the heavy things that you cannot bear; give it all to Jesus and know that he does care.

This man who was once perfect and totally without blame, he shed his blood for us, he took upon our shame.

True Christians who have faith and who truly live by the word, lift your voices as loud as you can and spread God's love and be heard.

This world can act as it wants to. But as for me and my house, we will serve the Lord, for that's what we choose to do. My voice will be boisterous, not like a mouse; yes, we will serve our Lord. How about you?

(January 8, 2012)

Give Him a Chance

I hold on tight wherever I go because it's the love of Jesus that lets me know that I am well taken care of.

Sometimes I want to shout from the rooftops about Jesus and his love, because he is honest and truthful in everything he does.

He has never let us down nor has he ever told us a lie; he had been so honest and open that sometimes he makes people cry.

All he wants from us is for us to be loving, honest, and kind; if you ask him to be your Savior then he will always ease your mind.

Just rest all you cares upon him, whether in good times or in bad, for he can fix any problem so you no longer have to feel sad.

(January 18, 2012)

Just to Let Him Know

God knows my name, he knows every bit of me, he knows every hair on my head, he knew when I was set free.

I was brought out of bondage with my own cross to bear; times were hard, but with his help to carry my cross, I know Jesus is always right there.

I still call upon Jesus and I count on him for every little thing, and that is why I will live or die for him, and it is his love that I sing.

I love to sing praises to him because he lifts me up me so high; someday I might be blessed enough to see his face in the sky.

His voice keeps telling me to hold on tight and keep my faith strong; that is why I praise my loving Savior all the day long.

I will hold on tight to him with all my might and I will never let him go. And tonight, I felt I had to tell him of my love for him; I just thought it was something he should know.

(January 16, 2012)

Every Day as I Say My Prayers

Every day as I say my prayers I always hope and dream that you will continue to answer me; maybe not in words perhaps but maybe a type of telepathy.

For you know what is forever unsaid and you always know what to do; even on the days when my faith may be tested, I know I can still always count on you!

You give me strength and make my courage stronger; you help me to feel as if there is nothing that I cannot do, and I continue my strength and my faith because of my love for you.

And even as a father should, you still sometimes tell me no, but I believe it is because I still have so much to learn; so as my Father— never let me go.

I grow in faith and grace, and in love remind of me my heavenly rewards from above.

Because sometimes I am still small and weak and meek as a little child.

So love me and protect me while teaching me my lessons all the while.

And when I act like a spoiled and mean little girl, remind me of how others are surviving in this cold and cruel world.

And when the sun shines down to warm my face, let me always remember to live for your mercy and grace.

(December 29, 2011)

Things That I Pray from My Heart

There is no other place that I would ever rather be than to be in God's love and grace continuously.

There is nothing else that I'd rather do than talk to my Father and pray for you.

For each day that goes passing by or each moment that might be missed is an opportunity to revel in our Father's love and relish his silent kiss.

You know like when a soft breeze whispers through the trees, or when a flower blooms with the greatest of ease.

These are things that I pray from my heart will never be taken away or be torn apart.

(November 14, 2011)

A Thank-You to God

My dearest heavenly Father, I pray that you give me strength to go on each new day; I know that I can do it if you just show me the way.

I know this world is hurt and it needs to be reborn; only your love can turn it around; that's why I pray to you each morn.

I pray to you so much, and I pray for every little thing; I pray that you still keep me in the shelter your wings.

I just want to say I love you and I thank you for your grace; I pray that maybe someday I can see your heavenly face.

It's All about Him

When I look to the sky, what do I see? I see God's grace watching over me.

I feel the gossamer of angels' wings; I feel his love and so many other things. I know that if I ever need him, I need to just call upon his name, because he is always in my heart and that will never change.

I know that no matter how bad things may get, I just need to look to Jesus and try not to fret; I know that I'm never alone; regardless of how many steps I take, I know how blessed I am for mercy and for heaven's sake. My Lord and Savior, he lives inside of me; maybe that is why I feel so loved and so free.

(October 17, 2009)

I Received a Blessing Today

I received a blessing today; I woke up early to the sounds of birds chirping. I sat with my mother as she had her toast and tea, so I had a blessing today because I know that God loves me.

I had a blessing today because I walked my dog and got to see the glory of the Glory of the Lord shining inside of me.

I had a blessing today because as I bade the moon a farewell for now, I felt uplifted and I know the who, what, where, when, why, and how.

I had a blessing today because my Lord has shown me the very special person inside of me just waiting to be a blessing to others so that the world may see that we are all blessed. Thank you, Father, for a beautiful day!

(May 17, 2006)

Flowers

Flowers all around me; flowers of each and every kind; flowers remind me of God's love; if you seek it, you will find. Just like the changing color of leaves on the trees or the soft subtlety of a warm summer breeze, flowers make me feel all fuzzy and warm inside; they remind me of God's gifts that I don't want to hide.

Flowers, like God's love, are something that with everyone I want to share, like a good bowl of soup, or your favorite teddy bear.

Flowers, like God's love, are awe-inspiring and abounding and, like everything that God and Jesus has done for mankind, are truly astounding.

(October 31, 2011)

I Will

To you I will sing praises from my heart and my soul, because to you, Heavenly Father, I will give my all.

I will write Poetry to you and glorify your name; I will try to make you proud of me without bringing you shame.

I will look for your love in all things great or small because, Father, I know that your hands created it all.

I will tell people of the wonders that you do; I will show others the glory of you.

From every tongue in every nation I will testify of your destinations.

All I want, Father, is for you to be well pleased with me, or as happy as a father can be.

(November 7, 2011)

Heavenly Father, Tell Me a Story

Heavenly Father, tell me a story, a story that happened such a long time ago, when friends were truly friends and a person had no foes.

Father, tell me the story of Jesus and how you sent him to this earth to be born as a blessed child from a woman of a Virgin Birth.

Father, tell me the story of how Jesus wanted to change the here and the now.

Tell me, Father, how such a perfect man, who was clean and without sin, put on the impurities and iniquities of a people who rejected him.

Then also, Father, please tell me how a wonderful and awesome being took the sin from us to put on himself. Father, that man died for us; he had no money—he had no wealth. Tell me, Father, how a person as loving and humble as me can ever repay such a debt that Jesus died on the cross for all to see; tell me then, Father, if there is anything else I can do except be the humbly abiding and loving Servant that will always cherish you.

I am even so grateful that Jesus, my rock and my salvation who died for me, is still listening to and answering prayers after the pain he endured on Calvary.

If I had but a drop of his strength, I would do the same thing that he did; this is not just a passing fancy that I write; it is for Jesus a loving hymn.

For there is no choice, no mere words that I write, that will prove to him my love; I will just keep doing what my Bible says and spread the news from heaven above.

(December 18, 2011)

When You Look at Me

When you look at me, what do you see? A woman with a mental illness who wants to be set free!

Until you have walked a mile in my shoes, don't pretend to know what I go through or what I have to lose.

I've seen so many hardships and so much loss. But now I have a great life, but it came with a cost.

I can never please everyone, much to my dismay, so I just try to take life day by day!

Tomorrow is never a promised thing, and yesterday is already gone, but I feel like yesterday's battles have already been won.

I try to look ahead of me, and not live in the past, because today is a great day and now I have a love that will last.

So once again I ask you, please don't try to categorize me, because I am who I admit, and that's who I shall be.

(November 9, 2019)

Daddy

Daddy, it's been so long since you went away, but I miss you more and more each and every day.

I miss your grumpiness and I miss your hugs, but most of all, I miss your love.

I miss the times when I would cook for you and I miss our talks when I was feeling blue; I miss the times when I would clean your house, but I don't miss feeling meek and mild just like a mouse.

Daddy, there are so many things left for me to say; why did you have to go away? Because you loved me oh so much, that's who I am today. And Daddy, you are and forever will be in my heart, so you will never really go away.

(November 9, 2019)

❦

A Daughter's Love

Dedicated to William Lewis from Opal Blue.
I love you, Daddy

Only a daughter's love can lift up her daddy sky high, where only God can reach him, and yet know that he is nigh.

Only a daughter's love can wrap around her daddy oh so tight and admit the times she was wrong and tell her daddy that he was right.

Only a daughter's love can make me miss you more each day. I wish you didn't have to die, Daddy; I wish there could have been another way. I wish your body wasn't as broken as it was; I never wanted to see you in such pain, but I want you to know how much I love you and we'll see each other once again.

(November 9, 2016)

The Family

Only the love of a family can cradle you in tender loving care, because the family will always give you hope and peace that's not found just anywhere.

Only the love of family will try to help you to understand that we don't go through our lives by ourselves, but we hold on to one and other's hands. Only a family's love can turn a gray sky to blue; and I feel so very blessed honored and loved that I have a family that you're a part of too.

I know that whatever happens in life, I have a family to which I can turn; my heart feels light, my days look bright, so for nothing do I yearn.

I feel so very blessed for all that I have and all that I do, and not only does my family love me but I love all of you guys too. And Father, I know you also love me, and I cherish you as well; I feel like I'm the luckiest person on earth; from sadness I've climbed out of that well.

I love my heavenly Father, and he loves me; that's the way it is and the way it shall be.

(January 17, 2017)

A Son Not My Own

Jesse, you were not born of me, but I love you just the same, and that's something that will never change. I love you just as much as if you were my natural-born son; you bring joy to my heart; my emotions you've won.

I will always pray for you when you have left our nest, because isn't life one of God's tests?

You will have many trials and tribulations, but when you succeed in them, it will bring you much jubilation.

Jesse, I'm always with you even if I'm physically not there; just know that Mama O. loves you and I truly do care!

(January 8, 2012)

A Letter to Mom from Keith

Mom, Lynette is breathing my air, that is why I socked her and pulled her hair.

Yes, Mom, I took out the trash;

wait till after this movie, and then I will go outside and mow the grass.

Mom, the boys and I are going to town to have a little bit of fun, so can I borrow $20, Mom? Thanks, Mom, I gotta run.

Geez, Mom. I need a new car; can I borrow yours? Mine won't take me very far.

Mom, I need some money for school.

I know I have to help, and you know the golden rule.

Mom, look at me, I'm all grown up now.

I still need my Mommy; you better believe it and how.

Don't cry, Mom; we'll see each other again someday.

Don't forget to stop and smell the roses and make new friends along the way.

Mom, I love you more than life.

Never forget, Jesus isn't done with me, no, so now I must look for a wife.

My only hope is that she'll be as great

As my mother 'cause Mama loves me like no other.

I Know

I know that I am tainted by the ugly stain of sin, so I stand here before you today, Father, and ask you to let me enter in. Enter into my heart and unto my every thought; don't leave me by the wayside, don't leave my soul to rot.

Every time I think I have an answer for the things that I have gone through, I know now why; it was because I took my eyes off of you.

And now I realize that some of the things that I've endured were to bring me back into the fold; but all things were done out of the purest of love, and love is a beautiful action and emotion that never really gets old.

So what do you say, Father, when woe is me and I can feel nothing but all so sad, because, heavenly Father, I want you to know that you are the best of everything that I have ever had.

(March 13, 2017)

Bend an Ear

We are all children of God, so no matter how hopeless the case may seem to be, he wants us to trust and confide in him—for that's all he wants from you and me.

The bleakness and darkness that seem to reside in the closest and deepest recesses of our hearts and minds, is something for my heavenly Father that we just cannot hide.

For Jesus is our shepherd and he knows our each and every thought; he knows each hair upon our heads. Jesus knows us so very well, he even knows what's in our thoughts and minds; he knows everything that has not yet been said.

And still he chooses to love us and give us guidance in every way, and if our load becomes too heavy to bear, he is willing to carry us the rest of the way.

So, my friend, if you need someone to talk to, and you feel that my ears just won't do, I beg of you to talk to our Savior, for he's waiting to listen to you.

(December 16, 2011)

Jeannie Anne

My most precious Jeannie Anne, maybe you can't hear us, or maybe you can. Just relax and let God hold you in the palms of his hands.

Let the angels that are with you surround you in God's love; just know that all of your family adores you; you were bought by Christ's blood.

All your aunts and uncles, brothers and friends, grandpas and grandmas, cousins prayed for you to mend.

Just know that you are a precious gift given to us from our heavenly Father and you'll know no love on this earth, for there is none other.

When God took you home, now that you're with Jesus, no longer will you roam—my, what a surprise—and now that you're with Jesus you will and always look into his eyes.

You have touched so many lives in a kind and caring way, so today I ask all Christians to take a moment to pray.

(January 25, 2012)

Count Your Blessings

Oh what a beautiful day that God has gifted to me; I await to take a deep breath and to revel in all the beauty that is surrounding me.

Such as the beauty of my soul mate watching me as I was sleeping or my heart beating out a constant song while Jesus holds on to it for safekeeping. (My heart, that is, and my love.)

The beauty of my dog whom we so affectionately call Mommy or the beauty of Scripture when you suddenly have an epiphany and go "Oh, now I get it."

And I thank God, and the creator of Facebook, for friends and families who were once lost to us but were never forgotten, because without these little tools in life to help us get through and get to and get along, I think we would all be disheartened.

(October 15, 2011)

Jesus, Save Me

Jesus, come and rescue me from the terrible awful sinner that I used to be.

Jesus, please give me grace, the kind that comes from knowing your face, the kind of mercy that sets my soul free, because of the love you gave when you ransomed me.

Lord, let me feel your abounding love gift so precious; it can only be given from God above.

Jesus, please help me be the very best I can be, because you are the one and only that made me.

(November 25, 2012)

Trinity

My darling dearest granddaughter, although you don't know me very well, and you probably do not remember my face,

to me you are the cream of the crop and you are the icing on my cake.

Your Grandma Opie loves you oh so very much and I miss holding you tight and feeling your baby's touch and I miss you holding on to my finger with all your might.

I miss singing to you when everyone else was asleep, for these are treasured memories that I shall forever keep.

Please, my darling Trinity, do not be in a hurry to grow up so fast, for the days already go rushing by, and you cannot get them back.

When I realize how little I get to share and be in your everyday life, it causes my heart to be in pain and it brings my soul such strife.

Never forget, my little one, that wherever you go and/or whatever you do, Grandma Opie will be loving and watching over you!

Always remember to say your prayers, be thankful to God, and accept Jesus's love around you, because you are not only loved by all of us here on this earth but also by everyone in heaven too.

Please, my darling Trinity, do not be in a hurry to grow up so fast, for we all love and adore you and we always will, and these are the emotions that will last.

For now and for always, you are our sunshine and our light; we only have to look at your sweet face to make our days seem bright.

Charming

My husband, my lover, and my friend, we have a love that will go on—until the end!

Thank you for always believing in me when no one else would, for putting your heart into it when no one else could.

Thank you for always listening to me, especially when I go crazy and my thoughts run free.

Thank you for being there when I need a hug, and thank you for being there to catch me when someone burst my bubble.

Your love for me can be so alarming. Like I'm the beautiful princess, and you are my dashingly handsome prince charming.

(December 13, 2019)

Jesus

All my faith is in you, Jesus, because there is nothing that I'd rather do except praise your holy name because I truly do love you.

You are the rock of my salvation—you hold on tight to me when I start to fall; that is why on your precious name I will always call.

You give me strength when I am weak; you make the blind to see; I know I'll love you forever because of what you've done for me.

How many ways can I say thank you and how many ways can I show you I care, because, heavenly Father, I know that you are always there. I love you, Jesus.

(March 16, 2013)

Say Hello

Say hello to a better day, where Jesus is watching over you in every way.

Where angels are on your shoulders and whispering in your ears; maybe they are talking to you about things you may or may not want to hear.

Where there is nothing ever but blue skies all around and where the sun does nothing but shine and reflect in prisms on the ground.

Where happiness is only a heartbeat away; where Jesus's love will never lead you astray.

Yes, love is where you will find me in God's holy and most perfect Word, because his voice is the most beautiful sound that I have ever heard.

(March 1, 2013)

Yet to Be Discovered

When you want to laugh, then you want to cry, then you want to scream and you don't know why, take a moment and lift your prayers up to the skies.

Ask Jesus to help you, for that is what he truly wants to do, because he really loves and truly adores you.

He is our shepherd, and we are his flock; he is our salvation; he is our rock.

He is the reason that we are standing here today; he is the light of the world and he is the only way that we should believe in.

So when you are feeling frustrated and you're feeling sad and blue, send a prayer toward heaven, because Jesus is waiting to hear from you.

(February 27, 2013)

Forever Blessings

I know that Jesus is continually watching over me; I can always feel his love and grace for he sets my soul free.

From the wind that whistles through the trees to the faint perfume of flowers floating on the breeze, for the beauty of the mountains that stands so majestic and tall, I thank God for my blessings, because he made them all.

Now, because our Savior loved us, and he died on Calvary, he gave us all hopes, dreams, wants, and prayers, gifts bestowed upon you and me. So the next time that you see beauty, like a flower about to bloom, open your heart and invited Jesus inside, for it you will always have the room.

Remember that God created all creatures great and small, and for this we should always give thanks to God for our God, he made it all.

(September 8, 2011)

Better Than

Father, you are my salvation, you are the light in my darkest days. You always bring me comfort and hope with your gracious and loving ways.

The way that you lift me up and keep my head up high, you bring strength to my body and keep my eyes trained to the sky.

Father, I can see blessings all around me even though I sometimes tend to forget that this world is just an inkling of a blessings we have not received yet.

Let me always try to stay in your favor, and I pray to always bring glory to your name, for my gifts in heaven and here on this earth are never quite the same.

I would rather have your love and grace and search always to see your face, for the material things of this world don't mean that much to me. I would rather bask in your love and glory, because it is you who sets my soul free.

(September 8, 2011)

Faith, Love, and Charity

Blessed are the people who speak so eloquently and blessed are the people who dress so beautifully but blessed most of all are those who show charity.

Love thy neighbor as thyself and to thine own self be true; share your blessings with other because that's what God says we ought to do.

Tune your ears for listening and stiffen your shoulders to cry up on; Jesus does this for us, so this is a gift that we must carry on.

Be a helpmate to others, the gentle and kind; never forget the blessings of heaven—that is what Jesus has put into our minds.

Always be loyal, stay faithful and true, because God has something wonderful in his mind and he is waiting just for you.

(September 14, 2011)

Have You Ever

Have you ever been grateful to hear a little child's laughter? Have you ever been grateful for the here ever after?

Have you ever been grateful to see the rain pour down on a Sunday? Have ever been grateful to Jesus for showing you a better way?

Jesus says he is the light, the truth, and the way; that is why he is my best friend, and it is to him that I pray.

I never forget to thank my heavenly Father for the gift of light that was given to me; if it were not for the gift, I'm not exactly sure where I would be.

So let me take this time to say thank you, and I'm always grateful even if for the smallest of things, that is why the angels in heaven and on earth of his praises we sing.

(September 13, 2011)

Family

Home is where the heart is, no matter where that home may be, it is what keeps families and loved together for example you and me.

Home is where you'll feel God's love, smiling down upon you from Heaven above. Home is where you should always feel love, because family is God's greatest gift to us.

In a home there is sometimes chaos and mind blowing chatter, you might hear some fairytales of different things or learn about Happily ever after.

No matter what your home is made of—whether it be rock stone a mortar home is where God brings all chaos to order.

Home is where you'll find love, laughter and sometimes sadness, but as long as you remember to put God first, your heart will always feel gladness.

Home is and will always be a loving connection in my heart between God, Jesus and you and me. So no matter where you are, or how far away you roam, remember to keep God in your heart, because there is never no place like home, no—there is no place like home.

Written by: Opal M. Belieu
1-1-2012

My Baby, My Daughter, My Hero

From the first day that you were born, I always knew you would be my heavenly gift from God; you have made me such a proud mother that I'm writing this to you with love.

I have always been proud of you and have always backed you up and everything that you do. And now your new life begins—you will start something new. My love for you as your mother just gets stronger every day; it is only for success, happiness, love, and laughter to be a part of your life I pray.

I pray for many things for and about you every day, the baby girl, my boo, my daughter—there is something I think that today you should know; not only are you the greatest doctor in the world but today on your graduation day, you are now and will forever will be my hero.

(January 18, 2012)

A Mother's Love

Father, we have two sons who belong to Uncle Sam now. I put their fates in your hands because only you can protect them, and I know that you know how.

Father, our sons are still in training, learning to be the best that they can be, but I pray you hold them in the palm of your hand, for it is your love that they need to see.

Please, Father, take care of them and keep them safe; I beg this of you from my deepest faith.

When the training is done and they go off to the battle, keep them in your love and grace to not get slaughtered like cattle.

You know that if I could, I would in an instance take their place to be the part of God's plan to save the human race.

Remember always of our sons to take great care, because a mother's love, whether on this earth or not, will always be right there.

(January 19, 2012)

Happy 50th Birthday to My One and Only True Love

I have loved you since I was sixteen years old, but like the fool that I was, I let you go; but as a blessing, God brought you back to me. I guess we both had lessons to learn that would make us see how precious our love is.

I know you don't go to church, but you respect me in my faith; that is why every day God gives me with you makes me feel like I've won a race.

I love you just as you are; to me you have no flaws. When I look at you, I see nothing but perfectness, and if God ever gets tired of listening to me, in you can find direction.

You are my best friend, my knight in shining armor. I know I can turn to you when having a bad day; oh, and you are the world's greatest lover.

If you can't tell by now, I hold your love up high, because you send my spirit soaring so I can reach the sky.

(January 20, 2012)

I Love You, Jesus

All my faith is in you, Jesus, because there is nothing that I'd rather do, Jesus, than praise your holy name.

You are the Rock of my Salvation; you hold on tight to me when I start to fall; that is why on your precious name I will always call.

You give me strength when I am weak; you make the blind to see; I know I'll love you forever because of what you've done for me.

How many ways can I say thank you and how many ways can I show you I care? Because, heavenly Father, I know that you are always there. I love you.

(March 16, 2013)

This Is Me

O Lord my God, what do you see when you are looking at me?

Do you feel a sinner who needs mercy and grace, or do you see the lost child who wants to see your face?

Do you see this woman who is me, thanking you for my blessings because I've been set free?

Lord Father, I also thank you for my tribulations and trials; I feel as if I have come so far, especially for miles and miles.

Father God, please never leave me, please be by my side, because it is in your loving words and precious heart where I always want to abide.

(April 6, 2013)

A Goodnight Prayer

Father, as dusk falls across the land, keep us safely tucked in your loving hands.

When the moon rises to meet the velvet sky, wrap us all in your graciousness till morning is nigh.

When your flock is so tired and we need to rest our weary heads, let us not forget to say our prayers as we stroll toward our beds.

Let us first and foremost give thanks to you; let us be always in prayer for all that you do.

Then let us always remember our own blessings and let us be in thanks for all of life's lessons; and last but not least, let us all pray for each other because we give, we get, and we live for our Father.

He Lives

You can promise me the riches of all kingdoms and you can promise me the wealth of the sea, but there is no place like God's House, for that is where I always want to be.

For the compassion of his promises and the gentleness of his words, there never have been such a sweeter sound of his voice that I have heard.

Father, please forsake me not, but leave me always to find your love and compassion and gracious gifts of every kind.

There is no place that I would rather be than searching the Scriptures when he comes to me.

Then when my heart is lifted and I begin to forgive, I know it is all because he lives, yes, he lives, he lives.

(October 6, 2011)

Spirituality

I think that I have found myself and I may have finally found my spiritual calling, so here I go on my hands and knees, and it is toward Jesus that I am crawling.

Even though I am still not perfect and I know I will never be, I can only give it one million percent because that is how God made me.

To be a Christian is to be like Christ, and this is forever what I strive to be, but I can never be as loving, as kind, or as gracious as my Lord has been to me.

Each day as I awaken, I will put on my spiritual armor, and I will join in the battle, the Battle of Good versus Bad; and when the day is done, I will say my prayers and be thankful and grateful for all that I've had.

(October 29, 2011)

Sending Up a Medical Prayer for Healing

Father in heaven, whose love I keep, help me please to get some sleep.

Father, I pray you stop these weird hallucinations and help me to get to my destination.

Father, I'm tired of taking all these pills, I'm tired of the aches and pains and all the chills.

Father, I just want again to be a healthier me; why can't the doctors understand this, why can't they see?

Father, I try hard each and every day; help me to be healthy, once again I pray.

I am so tired, and I wish the medical mysteries would end, but thank you for listening and being my best friend. I love you, Father.

(October 19, 2011)

Know Where You Are

I know I will never be alone, no matter how far I may have roam.

For you are always with me, you keep me on the straight and narrow, you bring peace to my soul and make my spirit soar as if I had the wings of a sparrow.

You always uplift me when I'm not sure of the next steps that I should take; you leave me in awe and wonder, and I tremble in your wake.

You give me all that I need, above all others, and I give my love and faith to you, for I love you like no other.

Father, your love keeps me right where I need to be, and that is strengthening my faith and my love and devotion to you, because you so love me.

(October 18, 2011)

A Prayer to My Master Teacher

Father, forgive me please, for not opening my mouth up when I should and forgive me for not taking the opportunities given to me to spread the love of your word.

Forgive me, Father, if my thoughts or actions seem to go astray; forgive me for my simple mind that sometimes goes in other ways.

Forgive me please, Father, when it is all that I can do to read Scripture and speak to others who are so in tune and connected to you.

I want to be a person in whom everything I do, others can see your glory come shining through.

For me myself, I feel always that I am wrapped up in your love and I seem to hang upon every word you have spoken and everything you say. Maybe I can be a good enough steward to send some lost souls your way.

I know I'm not the greatest student, though I try hard every day; I need to stay focused on your love, tell people of your love, and pray and pray and pray.

(October 16, 2011)

Let No Man

Because of his love, he took stripes for me; he was beaten and flogged upon Calvary.

I will always stand tall, my faith in him will always reign; he is my Lord and majesty; in him my trust will remain.

When people ask me who is my father, I will hold my head up high; I will say my father is the Alpha and Omega, my Father reigns from the sky.

Say what you want of me, you can backbite and gnash, but I will never leave my Father; I will always hold on to his sash.

So you can beat me and curse me and kill me and gather my plunder, but what God has created no man can put asunder.

(October 2, 2011)

Repentance

Some people were born for different reasons; some can sing or cook or tell of the seasons. But God has a gift for all of us: if we would just open up our eyes, all hearts will be fulfilled, and the love will be supplied.

Some people may have it a lot harder than others, and I guess that is where the long-suffering may begin; but always be kind to the widow and give charity, all of what you have or just as much as you can.

Fear not that your prayers are unanswered or have fallen upon deaf ears, but have you as a God-fearing soul tried to give back to God throughout your years?

I know sometimes we are young and rebellious, and we do things we know we shouldn't do, but when it comes to repentance, well, then, brother, that is on you.

I have repented many years ago and even got down on my knees to pray, then I heard a loving voice say, "Confess me as your Lord and Savior." I did, and that's what changed my rebellious ways.

(February 7, 2012)

Would God Know Me?

If I gazed up to the night sky, tell me, what would I see? Would I see my precious Lord and Savior gazing back down at me?

Would all the infinite stars, in all their starlight, create such a beautiful picture to see; would I be held on to as a precious stone, or would I be counted as a monstrosity?

Would God my Father stroke my hair and tell me never to worry for he is always with me so I no longer need to hurry?

Would God show me love through his unending grace; will I ever see his loving face?

At times, I keep asking myself, am I really good enough? Do I have what it takes to be that tough?

Sometimes the sins and temptations of this world seem too heavy to bear; I just hope and pray that the love of Jesus and God's guidance will always be there.

I just need to reach out forward and grab for God's hand and let him lead me to the promised land.

Showing My God Some Love

I love you, I love you, I love you, I do. I love you so much and you know that it's true.

Because you lift me up, you lift me so high, your love makes me feel like I can touch the sky.

You make me feel like there is nothing that I cannot do, and it is all because of my love and faith in you.

I know I can call upon you in good times or in bad; you are always there when I want you to be, whether I am happy or whether I am sad.

So heavenly Father, I just wanted to take this time to show you some love, because you are *truly* my awesome God from heaven; you are my gift from up above.

(August 26, 2011)

You Are

Heavenly Father, I never get tired of singing your praises or lifting you up high, because you are the alpha and the omega; you are the fire in sky.

You are the sunshine in the daytime that brings such beauty and light; you are the moon that keeps us safe and warm; you tuck us in at night.

You are the peace that comes to us each day; by your warm and loving embrace, may we always strive and seek to find your most precious and holy grace.

You are all that is good and right in the world; it is your mercy I seek to find; you always give me so much, and I give you so little; you bring me piece of mind.

(August 26, 2011)

A Lesson from God

Want not the material things of this world, for there will never be, not even as good as gold, or the love between you and me.

I don't mean to make you suffer much, but I need you to understand that you shall not inherit nothing until you reach out for my hand.

I only want the best for you, as much as I can give; but you've got to place me in your heart for as long as you live.

I'm not going to promise you silver or streets that are made out of gold, but I will promise to you my love, even when you're old.

My child, these are the lessons that I must teach to you. For the lessons that you must reach, I know deep down in your heart that we will never be far apart.

(August 26, 2011)

What God Might Say to Us

When you feel like you've been stripped naked and are feeling that your life is bare, just reach out and touch me, for I am always there.

Fret not, my child, and let my love unfold upon you; trust in me, my child, and see what my love can do.

Let the blood of my Son guide you and give you peace of mind; abide in my ways and answers you will find.

Help me to hold you up and lift the cross that you bear; just put your love and trust in me and know that I will always be there.

Call upon me at nighttime or in the early morn, and never forget that it is because of my Son that all was reborn.

I must bid you goodnight, my child, but just for right now; never lose your faith or hope because I know that you know how

To believe in and honor me!

(August 23, 2011)

Teach My Son to Pray

Remember to pray and sing praises.

My dearest and precious son, he knows that you need him, and he is always right just over there; he is waiting for you to show him that you really care.

You have strayed so far from Father, and he wants to bring you back to him; because without his love and grace, it feels like you've lost a limb.

Ask him for his grace and mercy, but mean it from your heart; because Father is never far from us, we are never far apart; just reach out with your heart and ask for peace of mind, for the gifts that he gives us are wonderous of the Heavenly Kind.

So, my precious son, I say to you never go astray; just ask our heavenly Father to show you the way.

(August 26, 2011)

Travelin' Heart

Where are you, children, why can't I find you? Why did you go away? Just know that I'll be with you in your journey, your hearts, and every day.

We may be miles far apart, but I know you're all grown up now and you needed to make a brand-new start.

You wonder what this world has in store for you. Will it make you happy or will it make you blue?

Will you be the superhero defeating evil at every turn, or will you go out and crash and burn?

Just know this, you take my traveling heart away and come back home. Jesus will never lead you astray.

He Teaches Me

Sometimes I feel like I'm making no sense, and I'm feeling like I might be dense.

Sometimes I feel so agitated and that in turn makes me feel aggravated.

Sometimes I feel lost, dazed, and confused; we all have our crosses to bear, but it's up to you; never forget that Jesus is always right there.

Sometimes I feel happy even when not only ten minutes ago I was super sad. I know you are with me, Jesus, because you are the best friend that I have ever had.

Jesus, help me, take me by my hand, lead me, and teach me, and help me to understand.

Help me to know all there is to know because, my heavenly Father, I love you so, so, so much.

(January 16, 2020)

Look for Me

When the rain comes falling down and there is no one else around, look for me.

When the leaves on the trees sway swiftly with the breeze, and you're waiting for an answer while you're courageously on your knees, look for me.

Look for me when the snow is falling and I come a-calling, and then when I call you darling, please look for me.

Look for me look all around; this is my state, this is my town. Look for me far or look for me near; just know I've always been right here.

Look, look, look, and see; peek-a-boo, you found me.

Whisper My Name

When you come looking for me and I'm nowhere to be found, whisper my name on the wind, and you will find me coming around.

When the day has turned into night, and you feel like you are too tired to fight, whisper my name on the wind and know everything will be all right.

When the seasons start to change and your priorities need to be rearranged, whisper my name to the wind for we will always be friends.

And when darkness comes marching in, here we go again and again; with all the stars shining bright as black velvet covers the night, whisper my name on the wind.

So as the days go rushing past, in God we find a love that will last; here we go yet again, just open your heart and let love in, and still whisper my name on the wind.

(February 13, 2020)

The Past

Don't pretend you know me, because you know nothing of my trials and tribulations; you know nothing of where my tears come from; you know nothing of my jubilation.

You know nothing of my past and you don't know what drives me still today; you may have been part of my past but I had to send you away!

You were never any good for me, and everyone told me so; but there was once a space in time when I just could not let you go.

But now times have changed, and I'm back to being good ole me, the me that everyone loves so much, the me that has been set free.

I'm no longer in your bondage, I'm no longer under your spell, so you can take your "I love yous" and "I'm sorrys" on the fast track to hell.

I'm happy now and I'm blessed I made it through another one of God's tests. Now I have a great life; it's better than ever before. So as I bid you adieu, I hope you find happiness too, and this is where I walk out the door.

(January 25, 2020)

The Lesson

I used to say I'd see you in hell, but now you are forgiven; we have gone our separate ways, so now we're even.

To love with a bountiful heart is truly a wonderful blessing; I count my days as they come one by one, and that therein is my lesson.

On the Wind

Have you ever take out the wind seen the purple mountains' majesty?

Have you ever painted with the color of the wind or seen the colored hyes, the purple greens, yellows, and blues?

Have you ever stood up for the flag with your hand over your heart, then made a promise to God and say that you'll never be far apart?

Have you ever walked in the valley in the shadow of death but still came out a winner, and even though you fought like hell and you gave it your best, you are still just like a lost sinner?

Have you ever stopped to smell the roses of life or any other flower? I know that when I do, I feel like it gives me a certain power.

The power to be happy and smile each day, a wonderful day, and the power to spread happiness all along my way.

So if our paths cross in the daytime, for you I will send love to you from me in the wind as much as can be.

And if our paths cross into the nighttime, then you with ease send it on the wind and know that it came from me.

Jesus, Help Me

Take away from me this feeling of anxiety and instill in me a feeling of peace; take away all the bad thoughts and put in my mind at ease.

Take away all my what-ifs and all my maybe-sos. Then give me more energy, the will to get up and go!

Help to turn the nos into yeses, even hell yeahs, and I'll do so with utmost delight; in fact, I'd do it so much, I'd do it both day and night.

Help me to get more sleep so I can wake up refreshed; I know you can do this because I know that I am blessed.

Instill in me love, kindness, humility; the me be who you created me to be.

Heavenly Father

I love it when you take me by the hand and take me away to foreign lands.

I love it when you guide my feet and cradle me in your comfort when I weep.

I love it when you help me hold up my cross because sometimes it is too heavy to bear; I love just knowing that you are there.

I love knowing the promises to my ancestors that you have made, and I know that because through them a lot of the promises will be obeyed.

I love how we walk together hand in hand, two in one, with only one set of footprints in the sand.

I love how you teach me, and some lessons are hard taught, and I love how you reach me, especially when I feel all is for naught.

How many ways can I say I adore you and I fear you like none other? I love you more than anything in this life, even my father and mother.

(January 24, 2020)

A Life's Lesson

I will raise my hands and sing his praise; may his love and mercy be upon me for the rest of my days.

Let not my heart be content with just his word; truly let the pen be mightier than the sword:

May I lift my head to gaze at the sky: to know for sure that my heavenly Creator sits upon high.

When I say my prayers but am not sure that he is listening, I get up early in morning to see the stars glistering.

When my cup seems so full that I can fit in no more, that is when my Savior opens up another door.

I only have to look at my family to see all of my blessing, but for some reason more than others, this is a life's lesson.

(October 25, 2009)

Blessed Be

Blessed be the earth, on whose surface he has trodden.

Blessed be the people whom he has never forgotten.

Blessed be the children who are missed by their mothers; and blessed are the mothers who are blessed by others.

Blessed are those who are actively seeking God's grace; and blessed are those who are looking for God's face.

Blessed are we the people one and all; because we have been touched by Jesus, we will not fall.

We should stand up and pray with our heads held high, not stick our heads in the sand while time goes rushing by. And be thankful and rejoice because Jesus will be there. Why, you ask, why does he keep on giving? It's because of his love that we are all living.

A Poem by Opal

My dearest heavenly Father, I come to thee in Supplication of Prayer, with thanksgiving, with a gladness of heart.

Heavenly Father, I sing these praises to you!

Father, thank you for the green of the trees, and thank you for putting my mind at ease.

Thank you, Father, for all of the flowers in bloom, and thank you for all of their sweet perfumes.

Thank you for all of the beautiful hues of reds, greens, golds, and especially blues.

Thank you, Father, for purple mountains' majesty.

Thank you, Father, for the blessings that you bestow upon me.

Thank you, Father, for the stars in the night sky; thank you, Father thank you for that twinkle in my husband's eye.

Thank you, Father, for all of my children, so courageous, beautiful, loving, and true.

Thank you, my heavenly Father, for all that you do.

Lest We Forget

To my heavenly Father, from one of your children

Have you ever stopped to see God's miraculous wonders? Have you ever looked at the blue of the skies or the green of the trees? Has it ever made you fall to your knees, and thank him for the beauty he has brought into your life? Have you seen all the beautiful birds that sing such happy songs? Have you watched the mighty soldier ants who are busy all the day long? Have you ever smelled the flowers with all their sweet perfumes? Have you ever wanted a house where God lives in every room? From the dew on the grass in the morning until the sun finally sets, we must constantly be in prayer and thanksgiving, thanks for all we get.

(April 29, 2009)

Doris's Garden

Oh, the beauty and the charm you will find on Aunt Doris's farm.

If you look hard enough you will find Cinderella's carriage, at least in my mind.

It's right there on that row of cucumbers, on the right, just behind the corn. It's a sight that can't be matched right here in the Garden Patch.

Come on over, neighbor, I might have what you need: corn, maters, or even green beans, but I don't have a trusty steed.

I have three ornery boys with a tomboy daughter to match, but they don't spend as much time now in our garden patch.

They've all grown up and moved on with their lives, and we are not as much a priority as we used to be, so I'll just be in my Garden Patch if anyone needs me.

But as the years go rushing past and the garden is no more, remember me with fondness as I sail out of life's door.

(August 24, 2017)

Happy Birthday, Jesus

Happy Birthday, Jesus, or so they say. Were you really born in December, or was it a March day with your love to guide me? I'll just be on my way.

We have been told these things all of our lives, and sometimes this causes me much strife

Because it really makes me to think and worry about the things used to be and it makes me wonder and worry what's in store for me.

Am I as good as I can be or should I or could I do better? I don't have the answer to that right now! So now I'm going to stop this letter!

(December 25, 2019)

Confusion

Massive confusion has come over me, and I feel so blind that I just can't see, can't see the forest for the trees; and all of this confusion is bringing me to my knees.

I wish there was some way to lift this cloud hanging over me and let the sunshine in and let happiness break free and let me be who I need to be.

And yet in my confusion, I still go on day to day hoping and praying for easier ways.

And I promise to love you all the rest of the days of my life.

(March 16, 1999)

Mother's Day

Mother, you are my mom and my best friend; you always lift me up when I'm at my end.

You give me the strength I need when I am weak; you know my thoughts when I can't speak.

You always show me you love me in the little things you do; that's why, my mother, I love you!

Happy Mother's Day!

Your Opal

I Love You, I Hate You

I love you, I hate you, I miss you, it's true; I'm so sad and lonely that I don't know what to do!

My days are spent in massive confusion; I'm wondering if the love we share is just some kind of grand illusion.

I hope for my sake that your love for me is real and your heart is honest and true, because if it's not, I just don't know what I will do!

This is love that is growing deep in my heart, so no matter wherever you may be, we will never be far apart.

(January 30, 1999)

I Loved You When

I loved you when I knew nothing about you; I loved you when you were sad and blue.

I loved you when you were down and out; I loved you when you wanted to scream and shout.

I loved you when...you were fired up...mad but you were the only true love that I ever had.

So tell me now, be honest and true, does any of this even bother you!

Well, guess what? I'm not in love anymore; my love had died when you closed that door. But guess what? I'm looking.

(March 8, 1999)

Fate

Love, laughter, happiness, anxiety—these are some of the things that you make me feel.

And whether you believe it or not, my love for you is real.

You can see to the very core of me, and sometimes I feel that you know me better than I know myself. So don't you dare put my love upon a shelf.

You are my shoulder to cry on; if I so need, your love puts me at ease.

We have been brought back together once again by fate and destiny, so every perfect world should have one of you and one of me.

He's Listening

When it seems that life has got you down when you try to smile but can only frown,

Lift your eyes and say a prayer; open your heart for God is near.

So when you're down and feeling blue, talk to God, my friend; he's listening to you.

(December 6, 1996)

Yogi

There once was a little bear who had lots and lots and lots of hair; he used to run from here to there.

Then one time this little bear asked his mommy, who was always near, "Why do I have so much hair?" Then Mommy replied, "My little dear, the reason why you have so much hair is because you don't wear no underwear."

"Oooh," replied the little bear, "I would be naked under there if I didn't have so much hair." Then the little bear said, "My name is Yogi and I'd like to say that I like myself hairy and all this way, so write this down in your history books today."

(February 26, 2013)

Someday

I am so sweet, I am so kind;

Sometimes I feel like I'm losing my mind.

I met two guys, both of whom seem too good to be true; I wonder, has this ever happened to you?

Where this will lead, who's to say? But hopefully I will find out someday.

I hope someday soon I will find happiness and true love, a gift especially for me sent from heaven above.

(March 8, 1999)

That's You

When I look at you, what do I see?

I see a kind, generous, caring man who I wish could someday love me.

Love me with all my faults and my disturbing ways; maybe if I pray hard enough, it will happen one of these days.

But whatever in my life comes to be, I will always be thankful for the kindness and honesty you have given to me.

Not for even one day will I ever regret the kind, loving person that I have met! And that's you!

(January 7, 1998)

Life's Test

All these feelings that I have inside, all of the raw emotions that I've been trying to hide, have been bottled up for much too long, so sometimes I feel like everything I do is wrong.

It seems like the everyday struggles become too tough to bear, and it leaves me wondering if there is anything better out there.

I hope someday the answers will find me and my mind will be at rest; but until then I will trudge onward, trying to pass life's test.

(March 19, 1999)

Take My Hand

I love you, I hate you, I love you, I do. I hate you so much that I'm terribly blue.

I'm so lost, dazed, and confused.

I think I'm just tired of being used.

I cannot be all things to everyone, and yet I don't want to be just someone to anyone!

Please take my hand and be my friend, and I'll cherish our friendship until my dying end.

(January 24, 1999)

All about Me

This is my story; this is my beat. I'll keep moving forward and running as fast as my feet can take me.

I try to live each day as the Lord has commanded me to do; I try to love my neighbor as myself—how about you?

I know I'm not perfect and I'm still a diamond in the rough—these are the things I keep telling myself, especially when times get tough.

To know me is to love me because I'm honest and true; tell me, have you sat down and had a hard look at your life—have you?

Now I'm not saying that I'm the best that has ever been or the greatest that will ever be, but when I step back and ponder about my life, I certainly like what I see.

(August 31, 2013)

Friend

I always said you were my true love, now I'm beginning to wonder if it's true; if God has sent me a second chance for love, and I'm wondering if that's you!

You are still and will always be my best friend ever, and for this I shall leave you never!

I hope you cherish our time together just as much as I do, because, my friend, if I don't get to see you every day, well...I miss you!

You know who you are, my friend.

(February 6, 1999)

Goodbye

All the tears that I have cried never seem to subside!

Whenever I think of you and what I've already lost. I vow to make my life better, whatever the cost.

So as I take the days one by one, you're still in my heart second to none.

I know we can never go back to what we had before, especially since I was the one to walk out of the door.

So until I die, I will always think of you, cherishing memories that were once new.

And now I can finally say goodbye with an empty heart and a tear in my eye.

Remember

Remember when we used to dance.

Remember when you took a chance.

Remember when you made you cry; that is when I wanted to die.

Remember when we could laugh out loud. Remember when you made me proud!

Remember when it was all said and done, the good times, the bad times, and all the fun.

Remember when I said goodbye, with love still in my heart and tears in my eyes.

Remember how it used to be when you were still in love with me.

But now it's over and in the past remembering and hurting over what I thought would last.

Saying goodbye is hard to do especially when I can't forget you!

(January 20, 2006)

What Is Love?

What is love? Is love an honest emotion or is it gained by simple devotion?

Is it a feeling deep within your heart that burns like a fire through to your very soul; will love ever set you free, or will love be there when you grow old?

Is love a feeling, or is a state of mind? Will love ever find me, or will it leave me behind?

I have loved and lost so many times before. Will love capture me once again or will it be never more?

(April 24, 2006)

The Past

Twenty years together, it seems like just yesterday when you told me how much you loved me in every single way!

Those days are gone forever; we'll never have them again. So remember me often and with love, and we can always be friends.

The abuse and mean times are over, even if you know that you were wrong.

When you play your guitar, remember our song! Remember how I tried to sing and make you happy with my songs.

Just missing you daily is where I keep going wrong!

My mind keeps drifting back to you and all the times we shared. I know that there was once upon a time when you cared; you cared so much about me, and all that I would say!

That is why I miss you each and every day!

(November 14, 2006)

Memories

Remembering the past and what you meant to me makes my heart ache, because it will never again be.

We have a long history of love together; we have precious memories that I will always treasure.

We've had a lot of good times and even some bad, but it will never change the love that we had.

We have had many ups and downs, but when things got really tough and you would never stick around you know where I could be found.

But I always came back because I loved you so and I still do.

I hope you still have love in heart for me, because once upon a time we were meant to be.

You used to make me laugh so hard I'd cry; then there were feelings between us real bad and I don't even know why.

I pray that I'm in your heart, you miss me so much that deep down into your very soul. Because what we had was truly real. Without me you will never be whole.

Remember when you used to love me and make me happy when I was blue; remember when you used to hold me until I told you that I loved you!

Remember when you used to always bring up the past; remembering now makes me cry for a love that I thought would last.

Remember when you kissed me goodnight until you took my breath away; being without you all this time makes me long for those days.

Remember us cuddling and me holding you tight even when you tossed and turned all night.

Remember when you had bad dreams and you would talk out loud; remember how I would soothe you and tell you that you made me proud. Proud to be with you and proud to be your wife, because that is what I always wanted all throughout my life.

(November 20, 2006)

From the Heart

A broken heart never mends, and rainbows never end. The love we have deep inside never truly dies; it manifests wings and learns to fly across great distances and across the sky.

Sometimes it's here or it's way over there, tugging at our heartstrings when were unaware. Deep in our minds, precious memories we will always keep, and the love that we have just settles way down deep.

Waiting for someone to unlock that door, flying with unbroken wings forevermore; finding a place of contentment right around you. I speak from the heart, so you know this is true.

(December 15, 1999)

Another Chance

I always said you were my true love, and I'm beginning to realize it's true that God has sent me another chance for happiness in the form of you.

You always lift my spirits when I'm feeling sad and low, and for this I am thankful, and I just wanted you to know. As far as best friends go, John-John, you are at the tops. Someday if we fall in love, I will never want it to stop and I just thought that this is something that you should know.

To you from me
Love always
"Opie"
(February 10, 1999)

Someone to Love

Father, send an angel to watch over me; show me things that I refused to see.

Show me that life really can be good without all the hassles of livin' in the hood.

Father, send me someone to love me true without the abuse that makes me black and blue.

Father, send me someone to cherish and love; make it feel so right, like a gift from above.

I know no one can love me as much as you do, but, Father, I need someone to love, yes, I do.

When I'm Alone

When I'm alone, my mind wanders back into the past, trying to forget about the love that I thought would last a lifetime.

I've cried so much, yet there are still so many unshed tears as my mind goes reeling back throughout the years.

The years of hurt and disappointment and the requited love that I so freely gave to you makes all the pain come rushing

Back to replenish itself anew.

I don't know how long it will take before I will ever trust again, but I know when the nights get long and lonely, I sure could use a friend.

Starting Over

I have a new life that does not involve you! But sometimes I still feel sad and blue!

I pay my own bills and make my own way, and as it was hard at first it gets easier every day!

Now I'm going on dates again and living carefree, and I'm only taking care of me.

I'm living my life the way that I want to, and every day is a great day. Because it doesn't include you, I'm paying my own way.

I will never settle for what I am given because I am a wonderful person that has a lot of livin' to do because I'm in charge of my life and it don't include you!

Maybe if I find someone special, I will be ready to slow down again, but for now I will do what I have to and make many friends.

(February 10, 2007)

My New Life

My new life does not include you or the things I miss about you.

I still think of you often and wonder when we went wrong; my love for you is still very strong!

I don't think I will ever stop loving you! Because you were the true love of my life; now I have to take it all in strife, and for now I am still your wife.

For you I will always care and have a deep love, because you were my hero sent to me from up above!

I hope you remember me with lots of love and tenderness, because I miss your sweet caress.

(February 10, 2007)

When?

The pain within my heart seeps deep down into my bones; when I will ever feel better? I'm afraid I just don't know.

When will my road less traveled be easier to trod upon; when will I find my true love! Tell me where is my "DONE."

When will the sunshine brighten my days again? When will the rain come pouring down? When will I be happy again instead of wearin' a frown? When will my heart find peace and love instead of bitterness and pain? Will I ever be able to love someone again?

I pray that I'll get through this a few steps at a time when can I claim true love to truly be mine? I want to be ready when love comes knocking on my door I'm already ready and I'll be grateful for ever more.

(September 8, 2006)

Broken Promises

As I sit here, I recall many of the promises that were made to me.

Promises like, I will always love you, or the promise he said when he said, I will never break your heart.

But you know it's going to happen, even from the very start. Because it's happened so many times before, you want to hit the ground running, until you can't run no more.

Now gone are the promises of everlasting love, hope, and trust; take back what little magic you gave to me; if you must.

There will always be a special place for you within my heart, so take my love with you, wherever you go, even when we're a million miles apart.

(April 10, 2000)

My Hero

I can still remember the first day that we met, that is one day that I never will forget.

You were wearing gray jeans and a black shirt and dress boots; I was wearing my shorts and a red shirt and my tennis shoes. I remember when I first saw you, you took my breath away, and I wanted to get to know you better but I didn't know what to say. I remember how all the women were tryin' to get your attention. But it was me that you chose to show some affection.

And then several years later, I found out that I was just a bet; but when it came down to it, I was the one that you just could not forget.

You said you fell in love with me at first sight, and I told you that you were right.

And then you would not leave the bar until I kissed you goodnight, and from that day on our love was a worthwhile fight. We have been to hell and back; we have gone through so much together that even if we are apart right now, our loving hearts for each other will last forever.

I Wonder

As I sit alone and ponder, it really does make me wonder how things came to be.

I'm sitting here while tears are flowing, not really even knowing why true love can't find me.

When you came into my life so many years ago, I thought life would be like a fairy tale; as if all my dreams could come true, you were my everything, my hero is what I found in you.

How long does it take for a broken heart to mend? Tell me if you can, does the pain even end?

So once again as tears are flowing and I begin to ponder, I sit here with my heart aching and all I can do it makes me wonder, Where am I going?

(September 1, 1998)

Waiting

As I sit here in massive confusion, thoughts of you are taunting me.

While tears are flowing and my heart is showing a love that keeps haunting me.

A once-vital woman with human desire sits alone and heartbroken, waiting for someone to rebuild that fire.

As the fog in my head starts to subside, I long for a place where I can run and hide,

Hide from the emotions and hide from the pain, not knowing if I will ever love again.

(October 2, 1998)

To My Children: Love, Mommy

I know I'm not there to hear your prayers and I'm sure I'll regret it in the coming years, but please be patient with Mommy for just a while because I'm trying to make things better for us somehow.

And if I don't get to see you but a few minutes a day, know in your heart that I'm paving the way for a better and brighter future for us all. So together we must stand tall.

And just remember at the end of the night, I will be tucking you in all safe and tight. I will hug you and kiss your brow! Because Mommy will make it better somehow!

I Cry for You!

At the end of an especially hard day, when I'm at my wit's end and can't find my way, I cry for you!

When the nights are so long that they turn into days, when I'm unhappy with the world and all of her ways, I cry for you!

When I'm especially lonely and I need to be caressed, and sometimes forget that I have truly been blessed, I cry for you!

When I want to run into your arms when I feel you can keep me safe from harm, I cry for you!

I cry for you sometimes, both night and day, while praying for an easier way to get on with my life; I cry for you!

Where Did I Go Wrong?

With unbroken wings I have been set free, because you no longer have control of me!

Now I live for myself and all the things that I can do, because I'm doing them for me and not for you!

Sometimes it's lonely and I get real sad, but then I remember all the good times we had.

I always remember you with love and kindness, even though you were mean to me and when you used to beat me up. You always said that I would always be the only woman for you, that I was your dream girl, but you're not supposed to treat the one you love in this way! So tell me, where did you go astray, when you were the light in my day and you were the lyrics in my song! So tell me, where did I go wrong?

(February 10, 2007)

Remember Me

Remember how it used to be when you still loved me; remember all the good times that we once shared!

Remember how I thought you cared.

Remember the laughter, the pain, and the tears; we were together for oh so many years! But you were the one who caused all my fears.

Remember the times when you told me stories about your past; remember the love we thought would always last.

Remember me with love always in your heart, because even if we're not together, we will never be far apart.

(February 10, 2007)

Remember How It Used to Be

Remember how it used to be when you were still in love with me!

Remember the looks that we used to share, when at the time you still cared.

Remember the things we used to say like, "I love you" or "have a great day."

Remember how we would say things that we didn't really mean, like "you should not talk but only be seen."

Remember how we would make love all night long, and then you would grab your guitar and play me a song.

Remember dancing to Elvis all throughout the night, and I could not do it, though try as I might.

Remember the nicknames we had for each other, like baby doll, true love, or my significant other.

I remember all these things every day and it makes me blue, because there is no way we can be together again, and it's all because of you.

(December 5, 2006)

All I Have Is Memories

I always think of you! When I'm alone and blue, I can't believe that we are no longer together because I thought the love we had was enduring and true.

And now you are with someone else and I cannot be myself.

No more happy, carefree days, no more laid-back, easygoing ways.

No more this and no more that, because I don't know where I am at.

No more spoiling you with all the little things that I used to do, because all I have is memories, but she's got you!

Now she has what once was mine, and I hope you are happy and everything is fine.

I will remember you always with love in my heart, even though we have grown apart.

(February 10, 2007)

Think of Me

In dedication to Terri Kisner, one of my best friends

Don't cry for me, don't say goodbye, I will be watching over you all as the years go rushing by.

Listen for my laughter that blows in the wind and know always and forever that I cherished my family and friends.

Look for me in the eyes of my little ones; this life has been a good one, but it not all been fun.

I've had some hard times, but I can honestly say I've made it through, but I never would have, at least not without all of you.

Look for me when the grass is green and the flowers are all in bloom, and then when you settle in for the night, blow me a kiss goodnight and say I love you to the moon—and back.

(May 28, 2018)

A Letter from Your Daughter to My Heavenly Father

Lord God, shower down upon me special gifts from up above, like the gifts of clarity, honesty, and love.

Lord, give me the gift of eloquence—to speak my truth whatever the consequences may bring, and Father God, will you stand beside me, guiding me through each and every thing?

Lord God, stand beside me as I stand against this world and have my say of what I believe in, because it is you, Lord God, that I love and I look for my say in.

I'd like it if the world would use more scriptures that somehow tie into the troubles of our day, because then I know we would be looking in the right place, and Heavenly Father would show us a better way.

Review and Ponder

Words cut like a knife way deep down inside; wounds that may or may not heal. I'm sorry but this is just how I feel.

Flashbacks in time that jolt out some memory or the way we had to live or things that happened to me.

Living on Parkay sandwiches or getting our first taste of bologna; these our memories that I ponder; all the time these are the memories that stick with me.

Being so poor that Daddy had to steal shoes for me, so I would have something that would cover my feet; going to bed hungry 'cause there wasn't enough food to eat.

Now I'm not blaming anyone for I believe this was my lot in life.

But still when I look back and review my distant past, it still cuts like a knife.

(October 3, 2013)

My Children

As you both wake up with sleep still in your eyes, I try to be happy knowing you are mine.

You say, "Morning, Mommy, you're happy today," I said today is gonna be a great day.

We've all kinds of things that need to be done today, and we are going to have fun along the way.

I will do my best to care for you and show you my love and be the best mommy, if you could just return the love back to me.

So when at night I lay you down to bed, and you smile and rest your weary heads,

I know I've done very best and passed through life's harder tests: my children.

(September 7, 1998)

A to Z Food

A—is for apple; they come in so many kinds: reds, yellows, and greens; would you like a bite of mine?

B—is for blueberries; they grow on a bush; you have to be very gentle when you pick them or they will turn to mush.

C—is for carrots; they taste good and sweet; put a little butter and brown sugar on them for an extra sweet treat.

D—Doritos; it's a potato chip made out of corn, you see, and now they have so many flavors for you and even me.

E—is for eggs; they come from chickens, you know; you can fry them, scramble them, even bring them to a boil.

F—frozen french fries; they're oh so yummy; they're easy for Mommy to make and feel good in my tummy!

G—is for gravy; it's good on mashed taters; gotta hurry, gotta say bye, Mom and Dad, see ya laters.

H—H is hot wings; they're good for any time, not just game day! Better buy a lot, 'cause I can eat like nine pounds by myself anyway!

I—is for ice-cream—*oh* how I love that stuff and always will in any shape or form; I feel like it should be part of everyone's norm.

J—is for jalapenos; they're hot and spicy, take it from me; if you don't believe me, bite into one and you soon will see.

K—is for kale; it's a green, leafy vegetable that's grown on a farm; it's good for you, tastes great, and if you eat it you can never go wrong.

L—is for lettuce; there are so many different kinds; you put them in salads; they're good for your body and minds.

M—macaroni; you boil and put cheese on it or put mayonnaise on it and cold, it's so yummy it never gets old.

N—is for noodles; there's so many kinds: linguine, rotini, lasagna, you want some manicotti; make some for me please!

O—is for oatmeal; it tastes real good and it makes you big and strong; one bowl in the morning will keep you full all day long!

P—is for pineapple; it's a sweet, juicy fruit; Hawaii or Mexico someday maybe that's a place where you can go—and pick your own pineapple!

Q—Q is for quesadilla; it's a Spanish bread with cheese and sometimes stuffed with chicken or steak; they are so very good, the people who make them don't get a break.

R—is for radishes; they are crispy, red, and hot; a lot of folks like them, but for me—I think not!

S—sandwiches; already made so many different kinds, it will blow your minds!

T—is for tomatoes on or off the vine, nice and dark red, I'll take two slices with salt on mine! Thank you!

U—is Uno; it's a candy, but eat it slow; it won't go far.

V—is for vanilla beans; you make desserts with them and they're really tasty, but slow down, don't be too hasty.

W—is for walnut; they're really good for you; they call them the brain food, and when you eat a lot of them, it puts you in a good mood.

X—is for Xavier soup; it's a new line of soup; I hear it's real good; maybe you should try it and maybe I should.

Y—is for yogurt; it's so yummy and there's so many different kinds; I like blueberry, how about you? Tell me what's on your mind.

Z—is for zucchini; it's a vegetable, you know; it's kinda long and green and it helps a garden grow.

(December 23, 2019)

Pizza and a Best Friend

Once upon a time, there was a little girl named Mei, and she said, "I'm sad because I have no one to play with. I feel all alone."

Then one day, Mei met a new friend, Ewe. They had such a grand time playing that Ewe asked Mei if she wanted to come over to her house to play some more as Ewe had to be home very soon! And they were still having so much fun playing games and talking about boys and reading books and watching TV that Ewe asked Mei if she could stay for dinner. "Your parents would call my parents." Mei said, "I would I like that; pizza is my favorite food!"

So Mei said she would, and Ewe's parents would call Mei's parents if they could.

And then just to prolong all the fun they were having, Ewe aske Mei if she would like to stay the night; she promised her mommy and daddy to be good and promised not to fight.

So after what was a fun day and night with her friend, Ewe walked Mei home. They promised to be best friends forever and would never need to roam.

People I Miss

I miss my son; I miss his wife

I miss my granddaughters, and I miss my life.

I miss my grandson and I miss Mama and Garbonzo too; is there anyone out there who is missing you?

I'm sure there probably is, you are surely someone: father, son, cousin, brother, and I'm sure they love you like no other.

So don't you worry and don't you fret, because this is my story; yours hasn't come about yet.

When it does so, I'm sure you'll have so much to say; so say it in a nicc way!

Me and Mr. B

I'm over the moon; I can't wait to see what kind of blessings God has in store for you and me.

It's a love story in the making that took twenty-six years long; it makes me want to do a happy dance and sing to you love songs.

We are alike in so many ways, yet slightly different in others; I think that had something to do with our mothers.

A loving touch or a bop upside the head, a feeling of peace or a feeling of dread?

Mommy, come back; please come back to me; we all miss you so much, can't you see? Well, at least my Mr. B is still here with me!

(December 29, 2019)

Doodlebug

Today you are my sister, the same way it has always been, but I consider you so much more than that; I truly feel honored, because you're also my lifelong friend.

I am not the same little girl who you used to wait for after school. I would like to think it was because you loved me, but I know it was just one of Mama's rules.

Doodlebug, I remember when you thought you were Evel Knievel and we'd jump through the old tractor swing; but you got into so much trouble and everything that it brings.

I always sat on the back of the bike, and the day we crashed, Garbonzo said something don't look right.

Garbonzo looked aghast.

So down the stairs Garbonzo flew; she was coming to get you!

To the right, to the left, to the East, to the West, all of your friends they did scatter because when Garbonzo pulled the handlebar out of my ear, they all knew what was the matter.

But look at us now, we're all grow up with children of our own. But when I think back to that day, I remember how high we've flown.

(May 7, 2020)

Pocahontas

As I travel through this land of my fathers, the wolves who are my brothers, they walk with me; and when the days are short and food is scarce, I know that darkness is trying to defeat me.

When Mother Earth sends my sister the Eagle to scout out for new places for my feet to trod, I make my bed beside the stream and I think "How odd" that for all stars in the sky that shine so bright, they are the spirits of my ancestors and they guide me by night.

My other brother who is fearless and true, you gave him the Grizzly and he's watching you too

The puma who is my cousin, my spirit animal, he watches every step I take; I respect him and he respects me; it's a mutual admiration for one another for heaven's sake.

The mighty oak tree and the towering pine, they keep me safe when the white man steps out of line.

The tree of the weeping willow, she is my grandmother, and she is stronger than other; she protects the animals and the people; she always has been this way since way back when, and she will continue to do this time and time over and over again.

The wind that howls or sometimes whispers through the canyons on any given day, you can paint your world with the colors of the wind or just sit silently and listen to what it has to say.

The snakes that come out are of no kinship to me; they are like the tricksters waiting to be set free.

The elk and the deer who struggle to feed their young and yet remain out of sight, we as human mothers and fathers can relate to their plight; sometimes we feel deep in our souls that some things just aren't right.

So as Father Time draws another day closer to another end, be humble and be grateful for we truly count you as a friend.

You may see me here or watch me over there, or you can listen to me teach a Native American prayer.

(February 14, 2018)

Love Me

The world is a beautiful place, simply because you love me.

The sun shines upon my face, simply because you love me.

The songs of the birds are sweet, a melodious happy beat that makes you want to kick up my feet, and it's all simply because you love me.

The little things that we took for granted, they really do mean a lot to me, like a love so strong, warm and tender, like the feeling as if I'm on a drunken bender… I thought I never really was looking, so I really failed to see. And it's simply because you love me.

Give me two arms that will hold me tight and keep me safe throughout the night. And keep me safe as time goes on; keep me safe from all harm just simply love me!

(June 2, 2007)

My Three in One

My dearest heavenly Father, you are my one in three; thank you for the love that you have gifted to me. You are my three in one, you are my one in three, you are the very best of me.

So many people have tried and are still trying to be like you, Lord, for we all fall short of the glory, that is why there is always a beginning, a middle, and an end to everyone's story.

There are many other things that people without authorities have tried to do, but we will still say our prayers and then leave the rest up to you.

Let us not be fooled by parlor tricks or by those who profess to do many wonders in your name, because without the Sacred Heart of Jesus, all and everything is not the same.

(March 16, 2013)

On My Mind

What more can I possibly do to show you how much I love you!

Should I write you another poem, should I sing you another song? My days are hard enough to get through because you are on my mind all day long.

I wish I had a handkerchief that could hold a thousand of your kisses; then when I'm having a bad day, I can hold it to my cheek and mouth and feel the bliss that I am missing.

No matter where you go and no matter what you do, just remember that someone special is waiting at home, just for you!

(December 5, 2015)

My Life, My Way

I am a new person with new hopes and dreams, with new goals in life and more means.

I still cry sometimes when I'm all alone, but then I just hop on the phone.

I make friends easy and I like it that way; it makes for better days!

But sometimes I just want to be held in someone's arms; I want to feel that love and security again; I want to feel a man's charms and loved like I'm someone's heavenly gift from above.

I know it will come soon, but patience is not my virtue, and it's hard for me when my heart won't let me let go of you.

(February 10, 2007)

Without You

I was once alone and very sad because I lost what I once had.

I had hopes and dreams of wonderful and splendid things.

I once was loved loyal and true because I once had you!

I thought you would love me until the end of time. I thought you would always be mine.

But oh how I was wrong, and now my days seem endless and long.

I feel like there is a permanent cloud hanging over me, with the sunshine just barely out of sight waiting to be set free.

I go on now each and every day, praying for a new and easier way to live my life without you.

A Diamond in the Rough

Thank you, sweet Jesus, for holding me in the palm of your hands and not letting me go and thank you for whispering in my ear and telling me you love me so.

Thank you for letting me feel your presence and your abounding love when I was so close to losing my own life, but I knew you were there because I felt you and I spoke to you even when the pain cut like a knife.

I knew you before, but I feel like I want to know you even better. You are always with me—still I felt that I had to write this letter. I feel like I know you a little more now…

I am still a diamond in the rough with many facets to be sanded down, but what I have to say to say to this world is: look at me, I'm better than ever, and I want to stick around.

A Love Song to God

Glory and praise sent to thee, my God, for not allowing me to cease to ever again be.

Yet my body is still badly broken, and I this child of yours you have not forsaken.

Yet to you do I sing glory and praise, and your love I do raise above all other.

I wear your love like a wedding ring, a beautiful and magnificent thing.

I exalt you higher than any other; I love you more than my father and mother.

I love you, Father, more than anything; yes, sweet Jesus, I speak of you, of whom the angels sing.

To Love You

Thank you, God, for each great new day, and thank you, Jesus, for showing me the way—to love you!

Thank you, God, for sending Jesus to be everything good in this world that I needed him to be; yes, thank you, God, for showing me how you love me.

Thank you, God, for being the light of my day; thank you, God, for showing me the way to love you!

Thank you, God, for always being with me and never letting me go, when all along it's been your love that I seek, even when I didn't know, thank you for loving me.

Sweet Jesus

Wherever I go, I know you are with me because there is so much more left for me to see.

With an angel on my shoulder and tons of faith in my pocket and a picture of Mamma tucked away in a locket.

With the sun shining down upon my face, I will walk so far; I will win this race.

I'm ever grateful and feel honored to be one of God's children, because I know he's constantly watching and listening over me and he's constantly challenging me to be the best that I can be.

As I am walking through this land, I can feel my Lord and Savior close at hand.

So no matter where I've been or wherever I go, sweet Jesus is always with me, and this I truly know.

(March 22, 2020)

The One

Thank you for being my beacon of light and thank you for making everything all right.

Thank you for the sun and the rain and thank you for all my emotions, the laughter, and even the pain.

Thank you for the sun and moon and the zillion stars above, but sweet Jesus, mostly I thank you for your love.

Thank you for your mercy, kindness, and grace, and thank you for always showing me my place.

Show me, Jesus, where I belong; teach me, Father, how to be strong.

Let me show kindness and love to others; let me love all others just like their own mothers.

May the mercy and grace that you give shine brightly through all those who cherish you and may you always be the one who makes everyone's prayers come true.

How Much Do I Love You?

I love you more than all the stars in the skies and I love you even more when those stars are twinkling in your eyes.

How much do I love you?

I love you more than purple mountains' majesty and I love you when you just want to hang out with me.

How much do I love you?

I love you all the way past the sun and moon and I love you more than all the flowers in bloom.

How much do I love you?

I love you so much that my heart is overflowing, and when you look at me you see me glowing; the sun is shining, a slight breeze is blowing.

How much do I love you?

More than life itself, that's how much I love you!

About the Author

Opal now lives in Boise, Idaho, with her husband, Mr. B, and her two fur babies, Mommy and Romeo. She loves planting flowers and tending to her memorial gardens, one for her momma and one for her mother-in-law.

CPSIA information can be obtained
at www.ICGtesting.com
Printed in the USA
BVHW030933200921
617094BV00001B/5

9 781638 811602